LEGENDS OF WARFARE

AVIATION

Fokker Dr. 1

Germany's Famed Triplane in World War I

MARK C. WILKINS

SCHIFFER MILITARY

4880 Lower Valley Road   Atglen, PA 19310

Designed by Justin Watkinson
Technical Layout by Jack Chappell
Type set in Impact/Minion Pro/Univers LT Std

ISBN: 978-0-7643-5968-2
Printed in China

Published by Schiffer Publishing, Ltd.
4880 Lower Valley Road
Atglen, PA 19310
Phone: (610) 593-1777; Fax: (610) 593-2002
E-mail: Info@schifferbooks.com
www.schifferbooks.com

For our complete selection of fine books on this and related subjects, please visit our website at www.schifferbooks.com. You may also write for a free catalog.

Schiffer Publishing's titles are available at special discounts for bulk purchases for sales promotions or premiums. Special editions, including personalized covers, corporate imprints, and excerpts, can be created in large quantities for special needs. For more information, contact the publisher.

We are always looking for people to write books on new and related subjects. If you have an idea for a book, please contact us at proposals@schifferbooks.com.

Acknowledgments

I would like to thank the following people for their invaluable help with this book: Greg VanWyngarden; Achim Engels, Team Fokker Schorndorf; Michael O'Neill, president, League of World War I Aviation Historians; Paul Daugherty, president, Golden Age Air Museum; Mikael Carlson; Chris Hill; Tom Polapink, Old Rhinebeck Aerodrome; Sarah Dunne, archivist; Sophie Gabrion, communications manager, Owls Head Transportation Museum; Ted Huetter, Museum of Flight; Steve Chapis, Golden Age Air Museum; and the staff of the National Archives, Still Pictures Branch, College Park, Maryland.

Contents

INTRODUCTION
The Rise of the Turn Fighter

Perhaps the biggest challenge for early aviation pioneers was the controlled turn. Many could glide or fly in a straight line, but only the Wright brothers could execute a controlled turn, thus giving their "Wright Flyer" the edge. Their wing-warping was widely copied in Europe, but those who tried in the US were embroiled in patent disputes; Glenn Curtiss dodged patent infringement by inventing the moveable aileron—it stuck and has been used ever since. In 1914, early exchanges between pilots were at first fairly amicable, morphing into progressively more violent interaction culminating with the Fokker E. III. This aircraft, by Fokker, could be termed the first modern fighter plane insofar as it was a "point and shoot" weapon: a machine gun sighted by the pilot and synchronized to fire between the propeller as he flew in pursuit of his quarry. Thus it evolved that an aircraft with the tightest turning radius would have the advantage, since it could "outturn" its adversary. For example, an aircraft that could turn inside another could bring its guns to bear via a deflection shot (the opposing aircraft would fly into the pursuer's line of fire). This began with the Fokker, Nieuport, DH 2s, and early Sopwiths and evolved to fighters such as the Camel, Fokker Dr. 1, and other nimble "turn fighters." The subject of this book, the Fokker Dr. 1, was one of the best turn-fighters of the war insofar as it could literally pivot on its axis in a very tight turn indeed. Its high lift coefficient and relative slow speed made it a quick but slow fighter that could outturn just about any fighter the Allies could throw at it—the Camel being more or less evenly matched at low altitudes. However, by the time it was introduced, the trend was already moving in the direction of fast, stable gun platforms such as the Spad VI and XIII, Fokker D.VII, SE5a, and Pfalz D.XII. The triplane was introduced a bit too late to see widespread use due to early production problems (wing failures), and the emphasis on speed instead of maneuverability. It was the last incandescent hurrah of the nimble turn fighter and is today perhaps the most iconic fighter of the war. It represented a final salute to the lone warrior astride his mount, battling one on one for control of the clouds. This type of dogfighting was already on the wane when the Dr. 1 finally hit the front in quantity. It was replaced by group tactics, codified attack methods, and increasingly faster and more-powerful aircraft.

The Wright Flyer was the first aircraft to master controlled powered flight. The Wrights' patented wing-warping system was copied by many—Bleriot's XI, Fokker's Eindeckers, and Morane's parasol fighters all depended on wing warping for roll control. *Library of Congress*

The Fokker Eindecker was an appropriation of the Morane monoplane. Fokker's big improvement over the Morane was the invention of the interrupter gear; this mechanism prevented bullets from hitting the propeller. Garros had fitted steel plates to the aft sides of his prop as a workaround to the interrupter system, but this was not a reliable or particularly good solution. Pictured is an E. III replica built by Achim Engels and flown by the TAVAS in Australia. The black-and-white image depicts an Eindecker captured by the French. *Image courtesy of Fokker Team Shorndorf, archival image Hélice Fonds Berthelé 49Fi608*

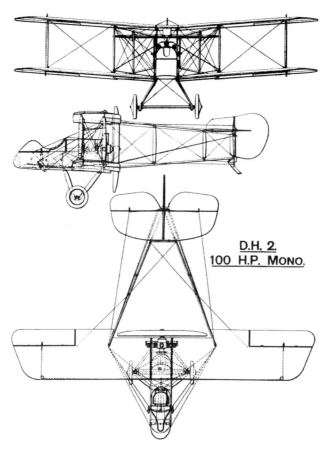

D.H. 2
100 H.P. MONO.

The DH.2 was another early turn fighter, and one of the last of the "pusher" fighters—an effort to work around the gun firing through the prop, by placing the engine behind the pilot. This system fell into disfavor, since in the event of a crash, the pilot would be sandwiched between the engine and the ground. That being said, in the right hands the DH.2 was a formidable weapon. Aces such as Edward "Mick" Mannock and James McCudden started out on the DH.2. *Public domain*

The Nieuport 11 was originally designed as a competitor of the Gordon Bennett Cup. After war erupted, it was hastily converted into France's first real fighter. It was nimble, had a good rate of climb, and solved the propeller/forward-firing problem by mounting a .303 Lewis gun atop the upper wing—thus firing over the arc of the propeller. Pictured is a Nieuport 11 from Escadrille N212. Its successor, the Nieuport 17, had a 110 hp le Rhône engine, slightly longer wingspan, and more streamlined cheek area and cowling. It also had an Alhemy interrupter gear and Vickers .303 machine gun that could fire through the prop. Pictured is the Nieuport 17 C.1 flown by Lt. Maria of N77. *Images courtesy of Philippe Guellermin*

155228 A.C.

This page and opposite: The Sopwith Camel was a contemporary and rival of the Fokker Dr. 1. It was an extension and improvement over the Sopwith Pup (*opposite*), in that it included two forward-firing Vickers machine guns over the Pup's one and concentrated all of the weight of the plane (engine, guns, pilot, and fuel) in the very forwardmost part of the fuselage. This enabled the Camel (in the right hands) to turn very swiftly—added to this, the gyroscopic effect of its rotary Clerget engine made very hard rights turns possible, making the Camel's turning radius extremely tight indeed. Training deaths exceeded combat deaths, but pilots flying Camels shot down 1,294 aircraft during the war—more than any other aircraft type. *National Archives, USAF*

CHAPTER 1
The Sopwith Triplane

Pictured is the prototype of the Sopwith triplane. The genesis of the Sopwith triplane was spurred by the desire for excellent pilot visibility, and maneuverability. It was created by Sopwith's chief engineer, Herbert Smith. Due to the narrow chord (3 ft., 3 in.) of the three wings, pilot visibility was good, which also generated plenty of lift. It was armed with one Vickers .303 machine gun synchronized to fire through the propeller (Contenesco system). The triplane emerged as a formidable weapon—especially since it could hold its altitude in a turn, whereas Albatros fighters could not. *Image courtesy of Greg VanWyngarden*

After triplane experiments by Hans Grade in Germany in 1908, in England by A. V. Roe in 1910, and in France by Goupy in 1908, the triplane fell out of favor, and the focus shifted to monoplanes. Triplanes had appeal due to the shorter wingspan that was possible by virtue of multiple wings; this attribute kept interest in the triplane alive. The genesis of the Sopwith triplane was spurred by the desire for excellent pilot visibility and maneuverability. It was the brainchild of Sopwith's chief engineer, Herbert Smith. Good visibility was achieved due to the narrow chord (3 ft., 3 in.) of the three wings, which generated plenty of lift yet afforded excellent downward visibility. The central wing was level with the pilot's eyes and as such obscured only the thickness of this wing. In addition, ailerons were fitted to all three wings, making roll rate very responsive and light. The fuselage and empennage were similar to the Sopwith Pup, but with different cabane strut structure (one wide strut port and starboard) to allow attachment of the three planes. The horizontal stabilizer had variable incidence, which was actuated by a wheel to the pilot's right. By careful trimming, it allowed the pilot to fly hands off! The introduction of a smaller 8-foot-span horizontal stabilizer and elevators in February 1917 made pitch response more stable and less "twitchy."

The triplane was initially powered by the 110 hp Clerget 9Z nine-cylinder rotary engine, but most production examples were fitted with the 130 hp Clerget 9B rotary.[1] The first Sopwith triplane (prototype N500) was first flown on May 28, 1916, at the test airfield at Brooklands by Sopwith test pilot Harry Hawker, who dazzled onlookers by looping the aircraft three minutes after takeoff. The triplane was very agile, with effective, well-harmonized controls. Due to the high aspect of the three wings, an observer commented that the aircraft looked like "a drunken flight of steps" when rolling.

The narrow chord aided maneuverability, since the shift of the center of pressure with changes of incidence was comparatively small; this permitted the use of a short fuselage. At the same time, the distribution of the wing area over three main planes kept the wingspan short, which aided in good roll rate. In July 1916, N500 was sent to Dunkirk for evaluation with "A" Naval Squadron, No. 1 Naval Wing, and was in action within fifteen minutes of its arrival. It won instant approval among pilots. The Admiralty and War offices were equally enthusiastic, ordering triplanes both for the RNAS (Royal Naval Air Service) and the RFC (Royal Flying Corps), to be produced by Sopwith, Clayton and Shuttleworth, and Oakley & Co. The second prototype, serial N504, was fitted with a 130 hp

Clerget 9B. N504 first flew on August 26, 1916. With this engine the triplane could climb 1,000 ft. per minute right up to 13,000 feet.[2] By September 1916, Albatros D.I and D.II aircraft had appeared at the front, posing a real threat to allied air superiority.[3] This prompted sending N504 to the front by November. At this time the RFC was struggling to ascertain what their premier fighter would be: the triplane or the fast and rugged Spad VII; they opted for the latter, relinquishing their orders for triplanes to the RNAS. This is why only this branch was equipped with Sopwith triplanes during the war. This also foreshadowed the direction in aircraft design for the rest of the war: speed. On the western front, RNAS triplanes were flown by squadrons 1, 8, 9, 10, 11, and 12.

The triplane was very effective in combat due to its exceptional rate of climb and maneuverability. Its service ceiling exceeded the Albatros fighters and was 15 mph faster, though the triplane was slower in a dive due to the aforementioned drag of its three planes. German pilots were stunned by the success of the triplane, such that they leveraged the Idflieg to develop one for Germany. This created a brief "triplane craze" in Germany, resulting in no fewer than thirty-four different prototypes, including the Fokker Dr. 1.

The Sopwith triplane's career was brief but extremely influential. Difficult to repair (the fuel and oil tanks were inaccessible without taking the plane apart), the triplanes required even minor repairs to be executed by rear-echelon repair depots. Spare parts became scarce during the summer of 1917, as Sopwith was tooling up for production of the Sopwith Camel.

Moreover, the wings of some Clayton & Shuttleworth-built triplanes collapsed in steep dives due to bracing wire that was too weak, which accelerated its obsolescence, and, like the Pup, the "Tripehound" also suffered from having just the single gun at a time when most German fighters had two.[4]

Triplane squadrons 8 and 9 replaced their triplanes with Camels between mid-July and mid-August 1917, and by the end of August, No. 10 Squadron followed suit. Although only 150 triplanes were built, they had quite an impact on aircraft design. Many triplanes and quadruplanes were built by top German and Austro-Hungarian aircraft manufacturers in an effort to match or exceed the performance of the Sopwith triplane. This phenomenon distracted the leadership and aircraft industry long enough to delay focus on the future path of combat aircraft: speed, stable gun platform, and group tactics.

Crew	1	
Engine	1 × 130 hp Clerget 9B	
Weights		
	Takeoff weight	1,541 lbs.
	Empty weight	1,102 lbs.
Dimensions		
	Wingspan	27 ft., 7 in.
	Length	19 ft., 4 in.
	Height	10 ft., 2 in.
	Wing area	264.79 sq. ft.
Performance		
	Max. speed	113 mph
	Cruise speed	106 mph
	Ceiling	20,350 ft.
	Rate of climb	1,000 ft./minute up to 13,000 ft.
	Range with max. fuel	280 miles
Armament	1 × 7.92 mm Vickers machine gun	

Pictured is Sopwith Triplane N5457 Flt Sub Lt. Hewitt, No. 1 RNAS, which was captured by the Germans. Unlike the Dr. 1, the Sopwith triplane was of conventional box girder construction (fuselage), with wire bracing. The wings featured the standard twin spruce spars fitted through ply rib webs and braced with antidrag wires set up on turnbuckles. The interplane struts were one piece and extended through the middle plane. The cabane struts were also one piece and extended through and became part of the fuselage structure. *Courtesy of Greg VanWyngarden*

Canadian Raymond Collishaw was the best-known Sopwith triplane ace—pictured is his plane *Black Maria*. Collishaw commanded "B" Flight of No. 10 (Naval) Squadron beginning April 1, 1917. It was composed entirely of Canadian pilots and became the famous "Black Flight." Between May and July, 1917, it accounted for no fewer than eighty-seven enemy aircraft. The original members were E. V. Reid, J. E. Sharman, G. E. Nash, and W. M. Alexander. The Black Flight planes were named *Black Death*, *Black Maria*, *Black Roger*, *Black Prince*, and *Black Sheep*. *Public domain*

Like all Sopwith and for that matter British aircraft of World War I, the triplane had advanced cockpit instrumentation and controls. It had a tachometer, an airspeed indicator, a compass, an air pressure indicator, a slip indicator, an oil pulsator, a fuel pressure hand pump (like many German aircraft), and a clock. In addition, it had a wheel to the right of the cockpit that allowed the incidence of the horizontal stabilizer to be adjusted in flight; the plane could be trimmed to fly hands free! The illustration shows the location of the various instruments within the cockpit. *Public domain; illustration courtesy of Rise of Flight*

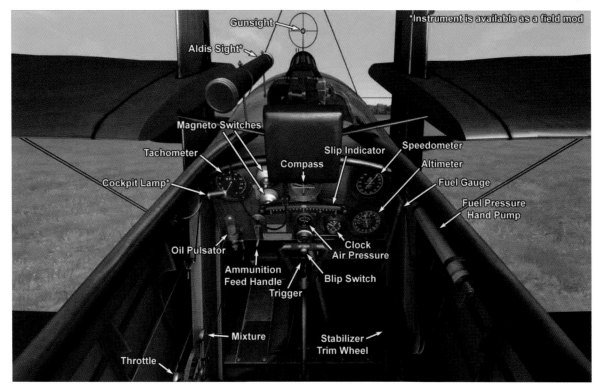

Pictured are triplanes of RNAS Squadron #8. The Admiralty ordered triplanes for the RNAS, and the War Office ordered 266 machines for the RFC. Naval Squadron No. 1's triplanes went into action in April 1917 to aid the struggling RFC, which was taking a beating by the German Albatros D.III fighters. The triplane turned the tide, outperforming the D.III—and shocking Idflieg (German Inspectorate of Flying Troops). The "Tripehound" could outclimb and outturn the Albatros D.III and was 15 mph faster, making it a formidable foe. Naval 8 and Naval 10 received their triplanes in April and May—augmenting No. 1's efforts. *Image courtesy of Greg VanWyngarden*

Pictured is a triplane that came to grief from a French naval squadron. The French had one naval squadron based at Dunkirk, comprising seventeen triplanes. In February 1917, the triplane was modified to include a smaller horizontal stabilizer and elevators, which made it easier to maneuver and dive, although implementing the changes was slow among operational squadrons. *Public domain*

The triplane was very effective in combat due to its exceptional rate of climb and maneuverability. Its service ceiling exceeded the Albatros fighters and was 15 mph faster, although the triplane was slower in a dive due to the drag of its three planes. German pilots were stunned by the success of the triplane, such that they leveraged the Idflieg to develop one for Germany. This created a brief triplane craze in Germany, resulting in no fewer than thirty-four different prototypes, including the Fokker Dr. 1. *Public domain*

This magnificent specimen is in the permanent collection of the RAF Museum in London. Clearly visible are the singe spars that pass through the middle wing and terminate at the underside of the top plane, and the top of the bottom plane. Also note the rigging—doubled flying wires and single landing wires. In addition, two antidrag wires were fitted forward (top of cowling to upper cabanes at top wing) to prevent the whole structure from rotating aft at extreme speeds (e.g., in a dive). Moreover, the Sopwith triplane featured ailerons on all three wings making roll control very sensitive and light on the stick. *Public domain*

This image of at least a dozen triplanes lined up on the flight line is of unidentified RNAS squadron. There are eighteen pilots/men standing in front of them. Some feature natural-aluminum-colored cowlings, indicating that they could be elements of Nos. 1 and 8 Squadrons of the RNAS. *Courtesy of the Canadian Air & Space Museum, CASM 6752*

Posing in front of this Sopwith triplane are presumably the pilot and a mechanic. Note the tie-downs attached to the base of each strut, which appear to be slack, indicating the plane is being readied to move or to fly. *Courtesy of the Canadian Air & Space Museum, CASM 8120*

This French postcard depicts RNAS Sopwith Triplane N6295 of No. 10 Squadron, which was stationed at Droglandt, France, during August 1917. *Image courtesy of Greg VanWyngarden*

This captured triplane, N5429 of Squadron No. 1 RNAS, is seen sporting German markings. This triplane served with Nos. 1, 8, and 10 Naval Squadrons. On September 13, 1917, Flt Sub Lt. J. R. Wilford of RNAS No. 1 Squadron was forced to land by Kurt Wusthoff. Following capture, this N5429 was repainted with German markings. The Vickers machine gun has been removed, and presumably this aircraft was subjected to rigorous testing by Idflieg and others. *Image courtesy of Greg VanWyngarden*

CHAPTER 2
The Triplane Craze

Spurred by the appearance of the Sopwith triplane at the western front in 1917, German aircraft manufacturers were prompted by Idflieg to produce a triplane. Pfalz led the way and by August 1917 was testing the Pfalz Dr. 1; this aircraft had an excellent rate of climb—reaching 5,000 meters (1,524 ft.) in 11 minutes, 30 seconds.[1] Manfred von Richthofen tested this triplane in December of the same year. On the basis of input from pilots such as the "Red Baron," Idflieg placed an initial order of ten triplanes to be tested in combat, which resulted in Jasta 73 at Mars sous Bourg receiving two Pfalz Dr. 1s (221/17, 222/17) in the spring of 1918.[2]

Due to production problems of the Siemens Halske Sh. III engine, less powerful 110 hp Oberursel U. II engines were fitted to the Pfalz triplanes, which were then termed Dr. II and Dr. IIa. To compensate for the reduction in power, the airframe was proportionally reduced, and, more importantly, the net weight was reduced from 510 kg in the Dr. 1 to 400 and 395 kg in the Dr. II and Dr. IIa, respectively. Unfortunately, the underpowered engine adversely affected performance, making the albeit lighter and smaller Dr. II and Dr. IIa more sluggish in the climb. However, the Pfalz triplane could outclimb the Fokker Dr. 1— the former reaching 5,000 meters in 19 minutes, 25 seconds, and the Fokker climbing to the same height in 23 minutes, 30 seconds.[3] In the final analysis, the Pfalz was not as maneuverable or production oriented as the Fokker Dr. 1 and, as such, was never put into production.

A flurry of fighter prototypes were produced through 1917 and 1918, as Idflieg raced against time to find the elusive "decisive weapon" that would ensure victory. This translated into the desire to find an exceptional fighter that could be mass-produced quickly. The resultant pressure was transferred to the aircraft manufacturers, who complied if they wanted a government contract—and they all did. Examples were produced by Albatros, Aviatik, Brandenburg, DFW, Euler, Fokker, Friedrichshafen, LFG Roland, Lloyd, Lohner, Oeffag, Pfalz, Sablating, Schütte-Lanz, Siemens-Schuckert, W.K.F, in Britain by Austin, and, incidentally, by Curtiss in the US at the war's end. Just one of many examples, the Albatros Dr. I was a German fighter triplane derived from the successful D.V fitted with three pairs of wings instead of two. Identical in most other respects to the D.V, in the summer of 1917 it was flown side by side with the existing biplane in comparison trials. There was no discernible performance advantage, and development was halted at the prototype stage. Only aircraft from Fokker were put into production. Germany was distracted by the Sopwith triplane when it should have been paying attention to the Spad line of fighters, which were fast, rugged, and foretold the future of fighter aircraft. Moreover, if Fokker had been allowed to pursue his V.1 and V.2 direction, he may have produced the D.VII or D.VIII much sooner. It is academic speculation as to whether this could have made a difference in saving Germany from defeat.

The Pfalz Dr. 1 was really the only competitive model challenging the Fokker Dr. 1. In some respects it was superior—it could climb faster than the Fokker triplane. However, it could not in all reality be mass-produced as quickly as the Fokker Dr. 1. In this image, a Pfalz Dr. 1 of Jasta 73, and the pilot stands near the tail. *Image courtesy of Greg VanWyngarden*

A close-up of Pfalz Dr. 1, 3050/17, with a familiar face in the cockpit—the infamous Manfred von Richthofen! The Red Baron was an enthusiastic advocate of the *Dreidecker*—such was his frustration with the inadequacy of the Albatros aircraft when compared to Allied aircraft of this period. In the first image he seems to study the instruments and controls of the aircraft; in the other, he seems just on the cusp of giving his signature smirk at the person shooting the picture. *Image courtesy of Greg VanWyngarden*

A view of the handsome Pfalz Dr. 1 from the front. Note the very narrow chord of the middle and lower wings, as well as the slightly forward position of the middle plane. No doubt, aircraft manufacturers experimented with wing chord and position to afford the pilot the best possible visibility. Also note the perforated cowling—an effort to enclose and streamline the rotary engine while simultaneously allowing sufficient cooling of the engine. Unlike the Fokker Dr. 1, the Pfalz had conventionally built wings and, as such, required rigging to support them. *Public domain*

Pictured here is a crude but effective test to see how much weight (drag) a wing could withstand before buckling or distorting. This process involved adding sand to various boxes or bags strategically positioned along a wing cellule structure. The Albatros Dr. 1 wing structure is the subject of the test in this picture. *Image courtesy of Greg VanWyngarden*

Pictured here is the Albatros Dr. 1. The fuselage is almost identical to the DV and DVa, and the wings feature a clumsy system of spars and wire bracing. The Albatros Dr. 1 had no performance advantage over the DV or DVa and as such was not pursued. *Image courtesy of Greg VanWyngarden*

The Albatros Dr. II was an attempt to produce a more production-friendly triplane. This sole example flew in the spring of 1918. It featured a Benz bzIIIbo engine, twin .312 machine guns, and wings of equal chord. The slab-sided fuselage with crowned turtle deck was an attempt to compete with the relatively easy-to-build Fokker Dr. 1. *Image courtesy of Greg VanWyngarden*

The AEG Dr. 1 never went beyond the prototype phase. Its chunky fuselage, awkward wing cellule, and stumpy appearance offer proof of the opposite of the axiom that "if it looks right, it usually is." Like the other triplane prototypes, it featured conventional wing construction and bracing, and, like the Albatros Dr. II, a slab-sided fuselage that was easier to build than the fully rounded fuselage of the Albatros and Pfalz Dr. 1s. *Image courtesy of Greg VanWyngarden*

The AEG PE or DJ I was a one-off ground support aircraft, a *Panzer Einsitzer*, or armored one-seater. It was rejected by Idflieg in March 1918 due to its poor maneuverability and performance. *Public domain*

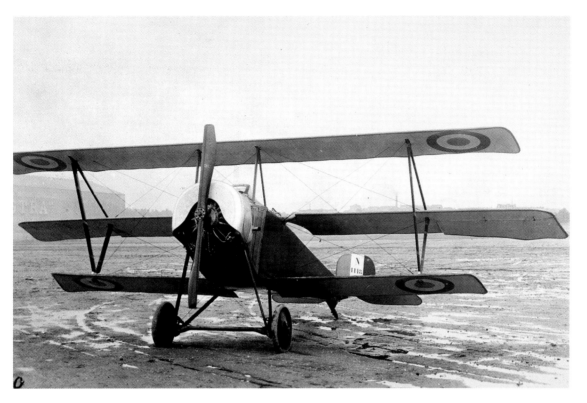

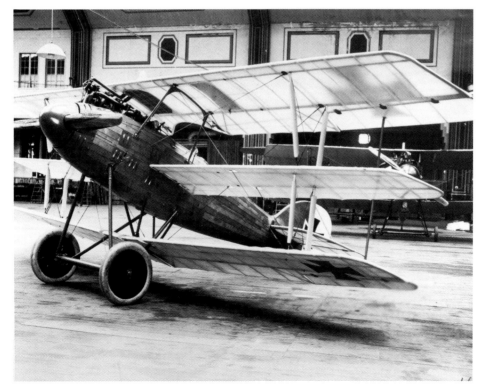

Allied aircraft manufacturers also participated in the surge of interest in triplane design. This image is of a Nieuport triplane, which featured an unusual design and nominal success. In most instances, triplane performance and ease of construction could not beat a given manufacturer's biplane counterpart. Certainly the Nieuport line of biplanes was proof of this, as was this one-off by LVG Roland. This plane featured progressively narrower chord wings moving from top to bottom, resulting in an approximation of a V strut. It had dihedral on the bottom plane only and, like so many others, was prohibitively complex to build for no real performance advantage. The D IV triplane was badly damaged after its testing in the summer of 1917, and development was then abandoned. *Public domain*

Although occurring much later than the triplane craze, America contributed the Curtiss S series, which was its attempt at a fast fighter. The S-1 (pictured in a parade in New York) first flew in March of 1917, as did the S-2; both these aircraft were largely unsuccessful. The S-3 became America's first triplane. One image shows it with a spinner. Compared to British and European aircraft of the time, it looks a trifle clumsy. It was powered by a Curtiss OX-3 engine. Note in the image the twin .303 Lewis guns mounted to the cabane struts! *NARA 165-WW-19C-26, 165-WW-19C-5; LOC N2014707556*

CHAPTER 3
Breakthrough: The Fokker Dr. 1

The genesis of the Fokker Dr. 1 was a complex and multifaceted story; an amalgam of influences contributed to the final design, including input from Fokker, Platz, Forssman, the Fokker team of designers, and Junkers that resulted in the Dr. 1. It began with experiments with cantilevered wings between Forssman and Fokker as early as March 1916; the latter instructed his chief designer, Rhinehold Platz, to build a prototype using these wings—the result being the V.1. Platz had contributed to the construction of two prototype biplanes in 1916: the V.1 and V.2, which had thick airfoils and cantilevered wings; the lower wing was a mere stub, and the Fokker team was clearly heading in the direction that would ultimately yield the D.VIII.

The Sopwith triplane made its incandescent debut over the western front in February 1917—Germany scrambled to develop an equal. In April 1917, Anthony Fokker examined a damaged Sopwith triplane while visiting Richthofen at Jasta 11, before it was taken to Adlershof for examination. He was also taken near the front so he could observe these planes in flight. Richthofen commented that the triplane was the best plane the Allies had due to its superior rate of climb, its maneuverability, its ability to hold altitude in a bank, its speed, and its ability to dive straight down.[1] The Red Baron and others in Jasta 11 wistfully acknowledged that the Sopwith triplane was better than their Albatros D.III. Fokker realized that he had been given privileged information.

Upon his return to his factory at Schwerin, Fokker instructed his design team and Reinhold Platz to build a *Dreidecker* (three wings) fighter, powered by a rotary engine, giving him only slight details about what he had seen at Jasta 11. Fokker insisted on the rotary due to shortages of in-line powerplants, and his controlling share in Oberursel engines, which could be produced with no limitations. Platz found the idea of a *Dreidecker* abhorrent, preferring instead to continue working on high-winged monoplanes—a natural outgrowth of the V.1 and V.2 aircraft he and the Fokker team had been working on. The V.3 followed, which included an Albatros-type tail, and the variable incidence of the upper wing was eliminated—and the increase of wing area from 17 m² to 22 m² on the V.2 was retained on the V.3.[2] Still,

the V.3 was better than the V.2 but couldn't match the V.1—most likely due to the overweight nature of the plywood wings and streamlined fuselage (921 kg and 938 kg for V.2 and V.3, respectively).[3] That being said, the V.2 and V.3 were better than the operational Albatros aircraft then in use.

Fokker, pressured by his knowledge that in June 1917 Idflieg was about to announce triplane contracts which would be awarded to three different firms, leveraged the Fokker designers and engineers to produce a triplane. They responded with the V.4, a small, rotary-powered *Dreidecker* with a steel tube fuselage and thick cantilever wings. These wings required no bracing wires or interplane struts due to the two parallel box spars joined with plywood webbing to form boxes within a box, over which the ribs were slid into place. The depth fore and aft of these spars eliminated the need for drag wire rigging, which was found on every other wing of the time that had smaller, solid-wood spars. The V.4 had an upper wing of longer span, and a shorter middle and lower wing of equal span. Fokker tested the V.4 himself, and after the flight Fokker instructed Platz to modify the next version to include balanced ailerons and elevators, and to add two sets of interplane struts—since the cantilevered wings flexed a bit too much for comfort. This resulted in the V.5 prototype.

Instead of submitting the V.5 for testing, the aircraft was rushed into production; an initial order of 320 aircraft was placed that included three prototype F.1s. On July 14, 1917, Idflieg issued an order for twenty preproduction aircraft. The prototype, serial number 101/17, was tested to destruction at Adlershof on August 11, 1917.

The first two F.1 prototype triplanes were serial numbers 102/17 and 103/17 and were the only machines to receive the F.I designation; these were distinguishable from subsequent aircraft by a slight camber of the horizontal stabilizer's leading edge. These two F.1s were sent to Jastas 10 and 11 for combat evaluation, arriving at Markebeeke Belgium in late August 1917.

Richthofen first flew 102/17 on September 1, 1917, and shot down two enemy aircraft in the next two days. He was very enthusiastic about the new triplane, and he told the *Kogenluft* (*Kommandierender General der Luftstreitkräfte*) that the F.I was superior to the Sopwith triplane—how he could know this without flying a Sopwith is perhaps wishful thinking. Richthofen recommended that fighter squadrons be reequipped with the new aircraft as soon as possible. The forward trajectory for the *Dreidecker* was halted when Oberleutnant Kurt Wolff was shot down in F.1 number 102/17 on September 15, and Leutnant Werner Voss, *Staffelführer* of Jasta 10, was killed in 103/17 after an epic dogfight on September 23. James McCudden and Rhys David claimed credit for shooting him down.

The remaining preproduction triplanes—now designated Dr. 1, were delivered to Jasta 11. Idflieg ordered 100 Dr. 1 triplanes in September, then an additional 200 in November. The Dr. 1s had straight leading edges on their horizontal stabilizers, and lower wing skids—the need for which became apparent after numerous instances of ground looping. In October, Fokker began delivering the Dr. 1 to squadrons within Richthofen's Jagdgeschwader 1 (JG or "group").

Compared with the Albatros and Pfalz fighters, the Dr. 1 offered exceptional maneuverability. Though the ailerons were nominally effective, the rudder and elevator controls were light and powerful. Rapid turns, especially to the right, were possible due to the gyroscopic force of the triplane's rotary engine and short-coupled fuselage. Franz Hemer of Jasta 6 said: "The triplane was my favorite fighting machine because it had such wonderful flying qualities. I could let myself stunt—looping and rolling—and could avoid an enemy by diving with perfect safety. The triplane had to be given up because although it was very maneuverable, it was no longer fast enough."

As Hemer noted, the Dr. 1 was considerably slower than contemporaneous Allied fighters in level flight and in a dive. While initial rate of climb was excellent, performance fell off dramatically at higher altitudes because of the low compression of the Oberursel Ur. II—the German version of the Le Rhône 9J 110 hp rotary engine. As the war continued, chronic shortages of castor oil made rotary operation increasingly difficult. The poor quality of German ersatz lubricant resulted in many engine failures, particularly during the summer of 1918.

The Dr. 1 suffered other deficiencies. The pilot's view was poor during takeoff and landing. The cockpit was certainly utilitarian if not comfortable. Furthermore, the aircraft was prone to ground looping and nose-overs due to its short wingspan and short fuselage and nose moment. Moreover, when the tail dropped on landings, rotating the middle wing downward, it blocked airflow from the tail feathers, making ground handling problematic. It was an aircraft that required expert and experienced piloting at a time when Germany was in short supply of the same.

Dr. 1 Specifications

Crew	1
Engine	1 Oberursel UR II, 110 hp, 9 cylinder
Weights	
Max. takeoff weight	586 kg (1,291 lbs.)
Empty weight	395–406 kg (895 lbs.)
Dimensions	
Wingspan, top	7.19 m (23 ft., 7 in.)
Length	5.77 m (18 ft., 11 in.)
Height, level	2.95 m (9 ft., 8 in.)
Wing area	18.66 m2 (201 sq. ft.)
Performance	
Speed @ sea level	185 km/h (115 mph)
Speed @ 4,000 m	165 km/h (106 mph)
Ceiling	6,100 m (20,000 ft.)
Rate of climb	1,000 m in 2.9 min. (3,280.84 ft. in 2.9 min.)
	2,000 m in 5.5 min. (6,561.68 ft. in 5.5 min.)
	3,000 m in 9.3 min. (9,842.52 ft. in 9.3 min.)
	4,000 m in 13.9 min. (13,123.36 ft. in 13.9 min.)
Range with max. fuel	300 km (185 miles)
Armament	2 × 7.92 mm Spandau IMG 08 machine guns

The genesis of the Fokker Dr. 1 was an interesting mixture of influences: part Anthony Fokker, part Rhinehold Platz, Moser, Forssman. and Hugo Junkers—the latter two were strong proponents for cantilevered wings, which profoundly influenced Fokker. Forssman introduced plywood as a viable building material for aircraft and was instrumental in developing the notion of the cantilevered box spar that would become a key component in the "V" series of prototypes, and eventually the Dr. 1. Within the Fokker company, many designers and engineers in the "experimental division" may have contributed in various ways to the genesis of the *Dreidecker* (pictured are Fokker, Platz, and Junkers). *Public domain*

This image depicts the V.1—it is just barely a biplane, with a large, cantilevered top plane, and stub—almost vestigial—bottom wings. It featured a rotary engine, the wings were sheathed in plywood, and the fuselage was completely streamlined—similar to a Morane Saulnier parasol monoplane. It was more akin to the later Fokker D.VIII than the Dr. 1. The performance of the V.1 would not be equaled until the V.4. Also pictured is the V.2, which basically was a version of the V.1 using an in-line 160 hp Mercedes engine, which was more available than high-quality rotaries. The V.2 featured unique control surfaces—the rudder pivoted above a stub fin, and the wingtips also pivoted in lieu of ailerons. *Public domain, and Fokker Team Schorndorf*

Pictured is the Fokker V.4, which is starting to look like the famed Dr. 1. It features three cantilevered wings with thick airfoils, and importantly the wings are covered in linen, not plywood, which proved to be a critical decision as it lightened the airframe enough to allow the underpowered rotary engine to produce decent performance. The control surfaces are unbalanced, and the horizontal stabilizer has a curved leading edge reminiscent of later Nieuports or Albatroses. The wings on the V.4 flexed a bit too much for Fokker's comfort, resulting in the fitting of thin interplane struts on the V.5. The V.5 also featured balanced ailerons and elevators to improve the "lightness" of the controls. The V.5 was the true forerunner to the Dr. 1. *Image courtesy of Greg VanWyngarden*

Werner Voss is pictured in the cockpit of the V.4 prototype at the Fokker factory at Schwerin during the summer of 1917. He was *Staffelführer* in Jasta 14 at this time. Voss loved the Fokker *Dreidecker*, and although scheduled to fly the Pfalz Dr. 1, he returned to the front to assume command of Jasta 10 in Richthofen's Flying Circus by the end of July. Voss was an enthusiastic proponent of the early-model *Dreidecker* and a superb Dr. 1 pilot. *Image courtesy of Greg VanWyngarden*

F.1, number 102/17, one of the first operational Fokker *Dreideckers*. Note the taper of the ailerons, inboard of which spans two frame bays; an easy way to spot early *Dreideckers*! F.1, 102/17, is seen outside a wooden hangar—something that Richthofen was outspoken about, since tents and exposure to the weather adversely affected these planes, as we shall see. *Image courtesy of Greg VanWyngarden*

Dr. 1, 152/17: the first number indicating the place of production of the triplane, and the "17" indicating the year it was built. This was one of the Manfred von Richthofen's early triplanes and featured the characteristic streaked olive paint scheme, to which the Red Baron painted the tail and cowling bright red. Also note that the ailerons have been modified in shape; the taper spans only one rib bay. This gave the ailerons more surface area and, as such, improved roll rate. *Image courtesy of Greg VanWyngarden*

Inside the Fokker Werke Schwerin, workers are seen painting the *Dreideckers*' wings with the previously mentioned streaky olive camouflage. Note uncovered wing structures in racks above, the covered and unpainted wings to the left, and completely finished wings in the distance. Wings were positioned this way to allow the natural dripping of paint to work to advantage, since this was consistent with the direction of the streaking. In the color image, a modern replica of a Dr. 1 wing showing the box spar, rib webs, antitorsion tape, and wing covering.
Images courtesy of Fokker Team Shorndorf

A Dr. 1 seen taxiing with the help of "wing-runners," whose job it was to guide the *Dreidecker* and prevent it from ground looping or spinning quickly one way or the other while taxiing. Also note the wingtip skids on the lower planes; since these aircraft were short coupled and high aspect, they were prone to dipping a wing and impacting the ground—the wing skids prevented costly and time-consuming repairs of torn wing fabric or damaged wing structure. *NARA 165-GB-9268*

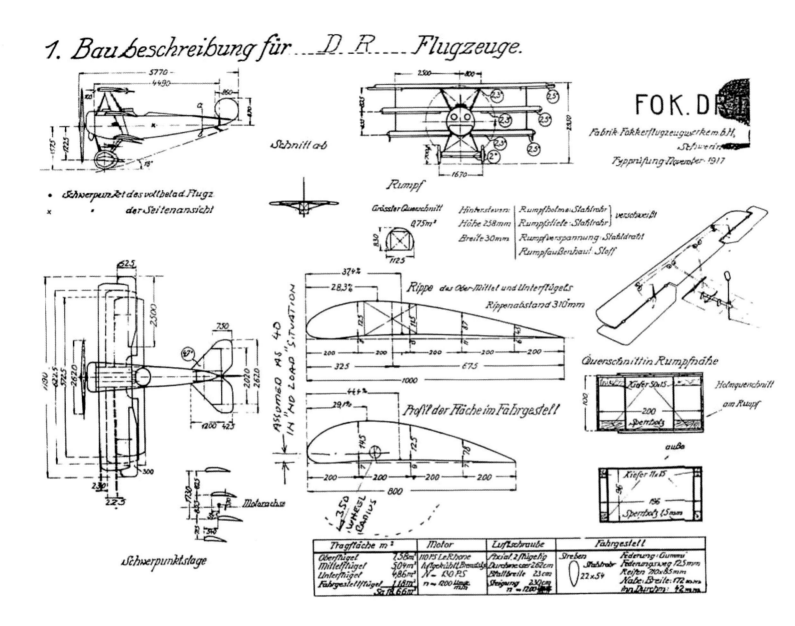

A drawing showing some of the more noteworthy aspects of the Dr. 1, including wing airfoil and landing-gear spreader airfoil—which generated enough lift to offset the weight of the undercarriage. Also, the proportions and construction method of the all-important box spar are carefully drawn. This spar made the cantilevered wing of the Dr. 1 possible. To the right is a sketch depicting the control line arrangement for actuating the ailerons—which on the Dr. 1 was on the top wing only. The Sopwith triplane (and other triplane prototypes) featured ailerons on all three wings. *Public domain*

Fokker F.I 101/17 landing, performing a low-level pass, or taking off. Opinions vary among modern pilots about the best way to land a *Dreidecker*; some prefer a "wheels" landing, while others prefer a three-point landing. However, everyone agrees that on takeoffs and landings, the pilot must pay careful attention! *Image courtesy of Greg VanWyngarden*

In this faded frontal view of the Dr. 1, 144/17, flown by Lt. Eberhardt Stapenhorst of Jasta 11, a very interesting feature is revealed: the port aileron is of greater surface area (a style employed by later-model Dr. 1s to increase roll rate), whereas the starboard aileron is of lesser surface area (old style). Perhaps this was an impromptu field repair, and matching ailerons could not be found. On January 13, 1918, Stapenhorst was forced to land due to antiaircraft fire, resulting in his and the aircraft's capture. The damage sustained by AA is visible, but not the rupture in the leading edge of the lower wing; also, the portside lower wing skid appears to be missing. *NARA 165-WW-22D-26, 111 SC 11859*

On November 15, 1918, just four days after the Armistice, the Royal Agricultural Hall in Islington hosted an exhibition of German military aircraft. For an entrance fee of one shilling, the public could see various captured or impounded German aircraft. Stapenhorst's Dr. 1, 144/17, was one of them and is pictured here. It was tested and scrutinized inside and out, resulting in the removal of the covering as seen in the image. Upon its opening by Lord Weir, secretary of state for the air, six airships and an entire squadron of Handley Page bombers flew in formation over the hall. Among other aircraft on display were an AEG reconnaissance aircraft, a Friedrichshafen bomber, a twin-engine Gotha, and a red, single-seat Fokker biplane, once belonging to the "Richthofen" Circus. In addition, a featured aircraft was an Albatross fighter plane in which Prince Charles of Prussia was forced down and captured in March 1917.
Image courtesy of Fokker Team Schorndorf

CHAPTER 4
Early Production Problems

Before the Dr. 1 could attain widespread deployment at various Jastas, it was plagued by problems with the wing structure. On October 29, 1917, triplane 115/17 came apart while being flown by the commander of Jasta 15, Heinrich Gontermann, who was performing aerobatics at 1,500 feet over his aerodrome. The Dreidecker was seen to lose control as the top plane disintegrated. Gontermann was badly injured and died the following day. Two days later, Jasta 11's Leutnant Pastor perished when 121/17's upper wing fell apart in a similar fashion. At this point, all Dr. 1s were grounded, and an investigation was ordered by the Sturz-Kommission. Richthofen was proactive such that even before inspectors arrived, he personally led an inspection of all triplanes under his command. It was discovered that poor workmanship had been the cause of the structural failures. Evidence of excessive moisture buildup had resulted in softening of glues, and delamination of joinery in box spars to rib joints. The Idflieg demanded that all Fokker triplane wings be modified, repaired, and made sound at Fokker's expense. In addition, tests on the shape and composition of the triplane's ailerons were also instituted by the Idflieg, which were inconclusive.

In response to the crash investigation, Fokker improved quality control on the wings production line (which was off-site at the repurposed Perzina piano factory in downtown Schwerin), particularly varnishing of the wing spars and ribs, to combat moisture. Analysis of glues used on the D.VII, after the war, indicated that a combination of hide (gelatin) and casein glues were used on the D.VII wings. Hide glue is water soluble, and heat accelerates this effect. If this adhesive system was also used on the Dr. 1, and the weather while these wings were being produced was warm and humid and the wings were stored, transported, and hangared in similar conditions, it may have exacerbated this flaw (in fact, Richthofen demanded wooden hangars for his Jastas). Fokker also strengthened the rib structures and the attachment of auxiliary spars to the ribs. He also modified the way in which the fabric covering was attached to the rib webs; originally the covering was nailed, but after the crashes it was stitched to the ribs. Fokker paid to have existing triplanes modified accordingly, and after testing a modified wing at Adlershof, Idflieg authorized the triplane's return to service at the end of November 1917, and production resumed in early December.

However, in spite of the repairs, the Dr. 1 continued to suffer from wing failures. On February 3, 1918, Leutnant Hans Joachim Wolff of Jasta 11 successfully landed after suffering a failure of the upper-wing leading edge and ribs. On March 18, 1918, Lothar von Richthofen, Staffelführer of Jasta 11, suffered a failure of the upper-wing leading edge during combat with Sopwith Camels of No. 73 Squadron and Bristol F.2Bs of No. 62 Squadron—he crash-landed and was seriously injured.

Postwar research and testing in 1929 by the National Advisory Committee for Aeronautics (NACA) concluded that the upper wing possessed a higher lift coefficient than the lower wings—at high speeds it could be 2.55 times as much, which increased the tension both on interplane and cabane struts. This combined with substandard craftsmanship helps further explain the upper-wing failures.

The delay caused by addressing and solving the triplane's chronic structural problems widened the gap between the era of the turn-fighter and that of the high-speed gun platforms such as the D.VII, Spad XIII, and SE5a. The bad timing sealed its fate as something of an anachronism and also eliminated any prospect of large scale orders. Production eventually ended in May 1918, by which time only 320 had been manufactured. The Dr. 1 was sidelined from frontline service as the easier-to-fly Fokker D.VII entered widespread service in June and July.

Heinrich Gontermann, *Staffelführer* of Jasta 15, was performing aerobatics at 1,500 feet over his aerodrome on October 30, 1917, when suddenly the wing was seen to come apart, resulting in an awful crash. Gontermann died the next day. Pictured are the remains of Gontermann's plane Dr. 1, 115/17. Note that the box spar appears intact (part of it broke on impact), yet the rib webs are completely stripped from the spar. Explanation of this phenomenon at the time centered on poor workmanship and not enough strength where needed, but modern testing suggests that the upper plane had 2.5 times the lifting power as the lower planes—resulting in stresses that may have contributed to or accelerated the structural failure. *Images courtesy of Greg VanWyngarden*

A close-up of Gontermann's cockpit—note the buckled tube steel framing of the fuselage, smashed windscreen, and apparently blood on the side of the fuselage covering. The machine guns stayed together as a unit and had padding on the aft side of the breeches to give the pilot some protection in the event of a bad crash. Unfortunately, in a crash of this magnitude, there was little that could be done to save the pilot. *Image courtesy of Greg VanWyngarden*

Another view of the upper-wing box spar, showing it devoid of any but the slightest trace of the rib webs, although their triangular attachment fillets can be seen. In the report on the crash, an eyewitness, Leutnant Arntzen, noted that as the plane slipped to the left and airflow was not only from the front but the side as well, the left aileron was seen to detach, and the breaking away of the wing ribs followed. The fact that the aileron actuating wires were rigged internally accelerated the destruction of the wing. Recommendations included diagonal bracing of wingtips and roots, as well as strengthening both of the auxiliary spar and its attachment (by means of triangular gussets). Further recommendations were to strengthen the balance portion of the ailerons and reduce the size (surface area) of the balance portion.
Image courtesy of Greg VanWyngarden

This image shows a replica lower triplane wing built by Achim Engels of Fokker Team Schorndorf. Note the attachment lugs near the wing root—for attachment and adjustment at the fuselage, the interplane strut attachment points near the tips, and finally the underwing skid attachment hardware nearest to the tips. Also note the diagonal bracing as advocated in the improvements by the Idflieg after Gontermann's crash. *Image courtesy of Fokker Team Schorndorf*

On March 18, 1918, Lothar von Richthofen (brother of the Red Baron), *Staffelführer* of Jasta 11, suffered a failure of the upper-wing leading edge of Dr. 1 454/17 during combat with Sopwith Camels of No. 73 Squadron, and Bristol F.2Bs of No. 62 Squadron. Richthofen was seriously injured in the ensuing crash landing but recovered. The images depict a plane that is more intact than Gontermann's, and certainly more of the rib webs appear to be attached to the box spar. Consistent with Gontermann's crash, there appears to be some buckling around the cockpit area.
Images courtesy of Greg VanWyngarden

Jasta 6's commanding officer, Hauptmann Wilhelm Reinhard, poses in front of his wrecked Dr. 1. His aircraft lost some of its upper-wing fabric in flight but was able to make a forced landing, which resulted in a nose-over. Most of the damage seen in the image was a result of the aircraft flipping, not an in-flight structural failure. The fact that wing fabric separated from the wing structure could have been from an increase in internal pressure due to a puncture of the leading edge in combat. Reinhard took over command of JG 1 on April 22, 1918. *Image courtesy of Greg VanWyngarden*

This blueprint shows the original Fokker rib web (*upper right*), which is composed of plywood and spruce cap strips. After the various accidents, Idflieg mandated new construction methods, which are described by the drawing of a rib web (*lower right*). This drawing shows vertical stiffeners of spruce to be glued between the lightening holes. It also shows the addition of a spruce stringer running through the rib webs near the trailing edge. Finally, the dash marks running along the inside of the contour of the airfoil indicate where linen tape is to be glued—to which the linen covering will be stitched. Originally, the covering was simply nailed to the rib webs. *Fokker Team Schorndorf*

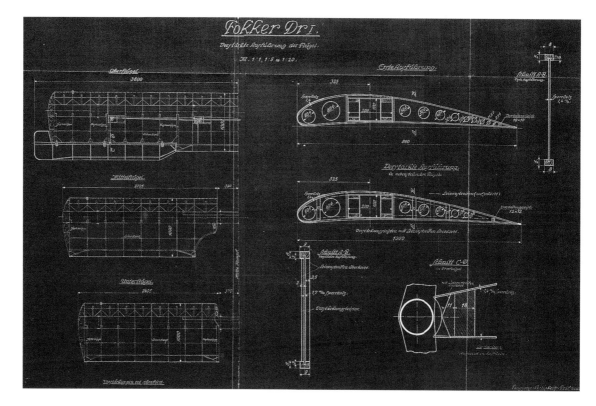

This picture shows the interior of the Fokker factory at Schwerin. The gentleman with the large mustache (and piercing eyes) facing the camera in engaged in retroactively rib-stitching existing Fokker Dr. 1 wings, per Idflieg's mandate that Fokker would repair at his own expense all existing *Dreideckers* to comply with new construction upgrades. *Fokker Team Schorndorf*

CHAPTER 5

Fokker Dr. 1 Aces

German pilots who flew the Dr. 1 well were also great pilots in Albatros, Halberstadt, and other aircraft that preceded the iconic Fokker triplane. The triplanes behaved differently from biplanes of the day in that they were quick but slow. They were very draggy and yet could climb rapidly, enabling those pilots who embraced the triplanes' positive attributes to attain a formidable presence in the skies over the western front. Due to the gyroscopic effect of the rotary engine, they could also turn rapidly on their axis to the right. Even though relatively few were built, there is no more iconic image (at least in popular culture) of World War I aircraft than the Fokker triplane.

Werner Voss was Richthofen's closest friend and was an excellent Dreidecker pilot—some say he was a better Dr. 1 pilot than the Red Baron. Voss had forty-eight victories to his credit and was due for leave. It would seem that something kept him at the front—perhaps an urge to bring his score to fifty before enjoying a much-needed rest. In any event, he took off on a lone patrol and became engaged in an epic dogfight with British SE5as of Nos. 60 and 56 Squadrons on September 23, 1917.[1] It ultimately boiled down to one against six, and British ace James McCudden was one of them. He recounted that "By now the German triplane was in the middle of our formation, and its handling was wonderful to behold. The pilot seemed to be firing at all of us simultaneously, and although I got behind him a second time, I could hardly stay there for a second. His movements were so quick and uncertain that none of us could hold him in sight at all for any decisive time."[2]

Hits were eventually scored such that Voss's triplane was seen to stop swerving and enter a dead-stick glide (perhaps he ran out of fuel), during which Lt. APF Rhys Davids got on Voss's tail and fired a final burst. Voss was buried by British soldiers where he fell, inside Allied lines north of Frezenburg.

Adolf, Ritter von Tutschek, was another triplane ace. Returning to active service in February 1918, Hauptmann Tutschek was given command of the new Jagdgeschwader 2, consisting of Jastas 12, 13, 15, and 19. He was pitched into the challenge of gearing up and staffing a new organization; he expressed his dissatisfaction with progress in his diary. The new unit was short of aircraft, parts, and fuel and faced a numerically superior Royal Flying Corps.

One of his prerequisites was a new airplane to fly. He was delighted with his brand-new Fokker Dr. 1 triplane. He first test-flew it on February 17, 1918, and raved about it in his diary: "a tremendous machine, climbs terrifically." He flew it to the last four victories of his career, on February 26 and March 1 (a balloon), 6, and 10.

On the last day of February, he narrowly survived a midair collision with Lt. Paul Blumenbach, flying another triplane. Both pilots managed to coax their damaged machines to safe landings.

Ernst Udet received the triplane (and his Pour le Mérite) after finishing leave in his hometown of Munich. Perhaps the most distinctive Dr. 1 Udet flew was the boldly black-and-white-striped machine of Hans Kirschstein of Jasta 6 (#586/17), to which Udet added his signature "Lo!" in red to the already striking paint scheme. It is unclear how Udet felt about the triplane, but he and his squadron flew the Dr. 1 throughout June 1918, before transitioning to the D.VII.

Joseph C. Jacobs, of Jasta 7, flew the Dr. 1 longer than any other ace.[3] He flew different triplanes, but the most distinctive of his mounts was painted all black with devil's heads[4] on either side of the fuselage (#450/17). He'd fly the Dr. 1 on low-level missions such as balloon attacks or when the clouds hung low, since the Dr. 1, like the Camel, was better at low altitude. Jacobs noted that the Dr. 1 was a very unstable gun platform, which required careful practice to master. It contributed to its short operational lifespan as Germany was running out of experienced pilots. Jacobs made his first claim in a Dr. 1 on April 11, 1918, but it was certainly not his last—it would appear as though at least half of his forty-seven victories were in triplanes.

Finally, although he shot down the bulk of his eighty victories in Albatros aircraft, there is no pilot more inextricably linked to the Fokker Dr. 1 than Rittmeister Manfred von Richthofen—his all-red triplane forever burned in the memory of all who are even vaguely familiar with World War I aviation and its anecdotes. Richthofen's "Flying Circus," so named for the brightly colored liveries of their aircraft, was one of the most famous squadrons of the war, and also one tied to the Dr. 1. The "circus" was an Allied moniker and was applied not only to Jasta 11, but JG 1 as a whole. Richthofen made the famous comment about the Dr. 1 as "climbing like an ape, and quick as the devil." He was keen to get the triplane to JG 1, since he had become frustrated with the obsolescent nature of the Albatros fighters relative to Allied aircraft. In all, Richthofen scored nineteen of his eighty victories in the triplane—continuing to use the tactics he had developed in other fighters. Opinions vary as to the character of the Red Baron. He took very good care of his pilots, but the expectation was on performance; any pilot who didn't measure up was transferred. The Baron rarely entered into engagements where he didn't have the upper hand. He was known to pick off stragglers and to retreat when facing unfavorable odds.

Lothar von Richthofen was ambitious and intent on catching up to his famous brother.

Werner Voss stands in front of his signature Dr. 1—the painted face taken from similar markings on Japanese kites Voss used to fly as a child. Voss was a gifted and precocious triplane pilot— some say he was better with the Dr. 1 than his best friend, Manfred von Richthofen. *Image courtesy of Greg VanWyngarden*

Jasta 12 Oberleutnant Adolf von Tutschek's Dr. 1, 404/17, Toulis airfield. One mechanic is preparing to prop the engine, while the other stands ready to hold the tail down after the engine fires. Note the wheels are chocked, and Tutschek is intent on checking the starter magneto or mixture/throttle setting. The portrait of Tutschek seems more candid than many of the images of fliers of this period; he seems to have been caught off-guard by the cameraman. *Image courtesy of Greg VanWyngarden, and public domain (portrait)*

Portrait of Ernst Udet, looking very posed in this Sanke card, was circulated in Germany to underscore the notion of the invincible German ace. Udet flew the triplane before his squadron and the rest of frontline *Jastas* switched over to the Fokker D. VII. *Public domain*

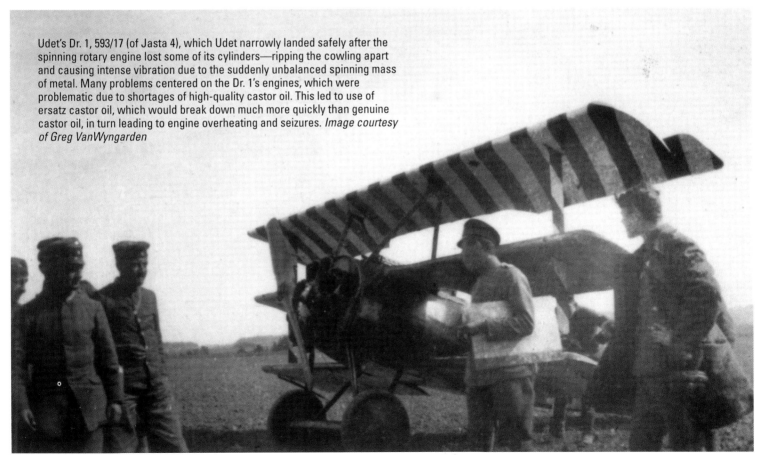

Udet's Dr. 1, 593/17 (of Jasta 4), which Udet narrowly landed safely after the spinning rotary engine lost some of its cylinders—ripping the cowling apart and causing intense vibration due to the suddenly unbalanced spinning mass of metal. Many problems centered on the Dr. 1's engines, which were problematic due to shortages of high-quality castor oil. This led to use of ersatz castor oil, which would break down much more quickly than genuine castor oil, in turn leading to engine overheating and seizures. *Image courtesy of Greg VanWyngarden*

Udet's Dr. 1, 586/17, of Jasta 4, at Cramoiselle during June–July 1918.
Image courtesy of Greg VanWyngarden

Two images of Josef Jacobs—one looking rather candid for a posed studio portrait, and the other as he climbs into his Jasta 7 triplane. Jacobs flew the Dr. 1 *Dreidecker* longer than any other German ace, piloting many different Dr. 1s. After the D.VII came into widespread use, Jacobs alternated between his D.VII and his Dr. 1, selecting the appropriate plane for a particular mission. The triplane performed at advantage at a low altitude; the D.VII, the reverse. *Image courtesy of Greg VanWyngarden, and public domain*

This page and next: Jacobs's most iconic and distinctive Dr. 1 was his all-black *Dreidecker* with a devil's face breathing fire painted on either side of the fuselage, which was Dr. 1 450/17 of *Jasta 7*. Note the Balkenkreuz crosses on the fuselage, upper wings, and upper surfaces of the lower wings.
Photo courtesy of Greg VanWyngarden; illustration public domain

Two images of Jacobs's Dr. 1 fitted with a captured British Clerget engine—this was done in an effort to improve performance over the factory-issued Oberursel II engines, which were slightly underpowered and fraught with problems due to lack of good-quality lubricant. *Image courtesy of Greg VanWyngarden*

Perhaps one of the most iconic portraits of the Great War—the Sanke card of Rittmeister Manfred von Richthofen—seen here with an calm, expressionless face staring seemingly right through the cameraman—seeming to epitomize German self-assuredness and determination. He is wearing his Pour le Mèrite or "Blue Max" decoration, which was the most coveted award for German fliers. On the right, an overexposed image of the Red Baron—there is just the slightest hint of a smile.
Public domain; USAF archives

Richthofen is seen visiting Jasta 5. A Jasta 6 Dr. 1, 525/17, is seen between the *Rittmeister* and others—
all of whom seem to be in good spirits. All countries during the war made a point to circulate the
most-successful aces to other squadrons, where they shared their expertise with fledgling and seasoned
pilots alike. Richthofen also used these instances to scout for expert pilots to join his *Jastas*.
Image courtesy of Greg VanWyngarden

The wreckage of Richthofen's Dr. 1, 425/17, which he was flying on May 21, 1918, when he was shot down and killed. Credit was originally given to Capt. Roy Brown of the RCFC, who did not respond well to what he'd allegedly done—checking into a hospital nine days later due to nervous exhaustion. Credit for the Red Baron kill was eventually given to Sgt. Popkin of the Australian army. Here is an excerpt from Brown's flight log of April 21, 1918, flying Camel B7270, regarding his encounter with the Red Baron: "Observed 2 seater Albatross shot down in flames by Lieut. Taylor. Dived on large formation of triplanes and Albatros single-seaters. Two triplanes got on my tail so I cleared off. Climbed up and got back to scrap. Dived on pure red triplane which was on Lieut. May's tail. Got in good burst when he went down. Observed to crash by Lieut. Mellersh and Lieut. May. Dived on two more triplanes which were chasing Lieut. Mellersh . . . Red triplane was Baron von Richthofen, confirmed by medical examination after being claimed by Australian RE8 squadron and 11th Australian Brigade." *Public domain, National Archives RG 165-BO-0986, Canadian National Archives*

This page and next: Lothar von Richthofen, brother of the famous Red Baron, was ambitious and driven to attain the same fame and notoriety as his brother. He appears somewhat smug and self-possessed in his portrait and is also seen climbing into his Jasta 11 *Dreidecker*. The color image depicts Paul Dougherty's beautiful replica of Lothar von Richthofen's *Dreidecker* Dr. 1 454/17, which forms part of the summer airshows at the Golden Age Air Museum in Bethel, Pennsylvania. *Public domain, Greg VanWyngarden, Stephen Chapis*

Hermann Göring in his Fokker Dr. 1, 206/17, of Jasta 27. He appears to gaze right through the cameraman, as if suddenly interrupted. Note the special spent-cartridge dumps under the main ammo feed. Göring is talking with other pilots either just before or after a mission. To the left, a D.VII; the triplanes were gradually replaced with the D.VII since it was relatively easy for new pilots to learn to fly, was a stable gun platform, and could be repaired fairly easily. *NARA 165-GB-9267.z; Greg VanWyngarden*

Göring and Jasta 27 line up for a group portrait in front of a lone Dr. 1. Jasta 27 was commanded by Göring from May 1917 to July 1918. He was an aggressive pilot and leader during World War I and was eventually given command of JG 1—formerly commanded by the Red Baron. Göring allegedly had twenty-two victories by war's end. *NARA 111-SC-9258*

CHAPTER 6
Museum Fokker Dr. 1s

Prior to World War II, there were three original World War I–era Dr. 1s in various museums in Germany. The last original aircraft, once flown by Richthofen, was on display in a Berlin museum when it was presumably destroyed by Allied bombs during World War II, although some believe that some of these planes were moved to neighboring countries. All of the Dr. 1s currently housed in various museum collections worldwide are replicas or reproductions. They all vary in quality due to the varying degrees of talent possessed by those who built them. In addition, a build can be only as good as the information it is based on; finding original plans is perhaps the best first step in building a replica aircraft. Fortunately, there are pieces of information that exist in the archives of other countries and trade journals of the time, such as *Flight*, *L'Aerophile*, and others. Jim Kiger, in California, runs Replicraft Plans Service, whose sole purpose is to produce plans of World War I aircraft that can be used to build replica or reproduction aircraft—"replica" being an exact copy, and "reproduction" being an approximation, although opinions on these two definitions vary as well. Finally, there is a fairly good network of people out there who have spent many hours researching fragments of original documents and talking to other enthusiasts about various aspects of Dr. 1 design and construction—many of the people mentioned in the next chapter are experts in this regard.

The Museum of Flight
Seattle, Washington

The Museum of Flight is located in Seattle, Washington, and museum staff described their institution as such: "Founded in 1965, the independent, nonprofit Museum of Flight is one of the largest air and space museums in the world, serving 600,000 visitors annually. The museum's collection includes more than 160 historically significant airplanes and spacecraft, from the first fighter plane (1914) to today's Boeing 787 Dreamliner. Attractions at the twenty-acre, five-building Seattle campus include the original Boeing Company factory, the NASA Space Shuttle Trainer, and the only exhibit of the rocket engines used to launch Apollo astronauts to the moon. With a foundation of aviation history, the museum is also a hub of news and dialogue with leaders in the emerging field of private spaceflight ventures. The museum's aviation and space library and archives are the largest on the West Coast. More than 150,000 individuals are served annually by the Museum's on-site and outreach educational programs. The Museum of Flight is accredited by the American Association of Museums, and is an affiliate of the Smithsonian Institution."
From Museum of Flight website

This Fokker Dr. 1 was originally built by Richard "Dick" Coughlin of New York between 1958 and 1972. After a mishap, the wings were repaired by Dick and Brian Coughlin. It was purchased by Doug Champlin, who had Joe DeFiore restore the aircraft to become part of the Champlin Air Museum in New Mexico. When Doug Champlin passed away, his entire collection was acquired by the Museum of Flight in Seattle, Washington—where it is today. *Museum of Flight*

In this image, the museum's replica Dr. 1 is dramatically positioned as if in pursuit of its chief antagonist: the Sopwith Camel. *Museum of Flight*

In this profile view the Dr. 1 is seen above two Nieuports—one slightly below, hoping to sneak up on the Dr. 1's blind spot; the other, Zigomar, is displayed in a vignette depicting a forward airfield. Both of the Nieuports were also part of the Champlin collection, which Museum of Flight acquired. *Museum of Flight*

The National Museum of the United States Air Force—the oldest and largest military aviation museum in the world—is located at Wright-Patterson Air Force Base, near Dayton, Ohio. The museum collects, researches, conserves, interprets, and presents the Air Force's history, heritage, and traditions through engaging exhibits, educational outreach, special programs, and the stewardship of the national historical collection. While the majority of the collection is housed at the museum, one-third of the collection is on loan both to civilian and military heritage activities throughout the world. *Excerpted from the museum website*

The Air Force Museum at Wright-Patterson AFB is home to a Dr. 1 that was built in the 1990s, and depicts the Dr. 1 433/17 of Leutnant Arthur Rahn of Jasta 19. At the war's conclusion, Rahn had six victories—a couple of which were achieved in his Dr. 1. Note the absence of the typical white field upon which the fuselage Iron Cross is usually placed. Rahn was wounded in the shin and hand on July 17, 1918; in spite of this, he managed to fly his Dr. 1 back to Leffincourt and landed safely. Rahn survived the war and immigrated to the US in 1928, ultimately settling in Michigan.

Richthofen's Red Triplane

Hands down the most common of museum triplanes is the Red Baron's all-red triplane. It is perhaps the most iconic aviation image of the First World War, and an almost "must have" for many aviation museums. Only two of Manfred von Richthofen's *Dreideckers* were completely red—Dr. 1 425/17 and Dr. 1 152/17. The following are a selection of the Baron's triplanes that can be seen in the US as well as abroad.

The Belgian Air Museum

The Royal Museum of the Armed Forces and Military History) replica of Dr. 1 425/17 was constructed by one Mr. Vandenberghe in 1976. The aircraft is completely functional, with a working engine. In 1983, the BAM and the AELR renewed and restored the fuselage and wings. Johan Slingers and volunteers from the AELR completed the final details and the paint scheme. The fabrication of the engine cowling was subcontracted to others. The completed aircraft was offered to the museum in January 1984; it was accepted and now hangs in the exhibition gallery 14–18. *Public domain*

Fantasy of Flight Museum

Located in Florida, this museum is home to a replica of another example of Dr. 1 425/17, which was acquired by the museum in 2004 as an unfinished project that featured a modern Warner radial engine. Apparently the aircraft's end use was for movie work. Kermit Weeks, founder of Fantasy of Flight, noted that the aircraft will be fitted with a rotary engine in the future. Weeks also commented that "The Red Baron and his red triplane had a very big impact on my early life that set me on a path to eventually create Fantasy of Flight Museum" (from Fantasy of Flight website). *Public domain*

The New England Air Museum

This Dr. 1 is on loan from the Old Rhinebeck Aerodrome, in New York. It features an original Oberursel II engine (which is the German version of the Le Rhône 110 hp). It was originally built by Norman Hortman of Pennsylvania and was purchased in 1969–1970 by Cole Palen as a backup for N3221. It was originally equipped with a radial engine, and Cole's goal was to replace the radial with a rotary to use in the shows, but there were complications switching the engines over, and the project was sidelined. It was displayed in the museum at Old Rhinebeck until the 1980s and was then loaned to the New England Air Museum, where it is today.
Public domain

Luftwaffe Museum Berlin-Gatow

The museum is located at Flugplatz Gatow 33, 14089 Berlin, and admission is free. This museum's Fokker Dr. 1 is located inside Hangar 3. There is an exhibition on the history of military flight in Germany since 1884. From their website (translated): "The museum is dedicated to collecting, exhibiting, and interpreting objects and cultural assets, since historical evidence is one of the most important functions of a museum, as is the preservation of such objects and assets. The Museum at the Berlin-Gatow airfield has a restoration hangar at its disposal in which up to four aircraft can be restored simultaneously. The restoration work is directed by a graduated restorer (technical control) and by an officer engineer of the Bundeswehr (organizational control). The workshops are staffed by aircraft technicians, varnishers, a female carpenter, a locksmith, and other specialists." *Public domain*

Technik Museum Speyer

Located on the Rhine, is home to this Dr. 1, which was built by Achim Engels when he was sixteen years old—it was to be the first of many triplanes for Achim (*see following pages*). It is a replica of Richthofen's Dr. 1, 152/17, which Achim built for the museum in his basement, attic, and garage—finally renting a barn where assembly could take place. Today, Achim continues to build excellent triplanes for people all over the world (see chapter 7). His craftsmanship is superb and his research into historical Fokker methods is exacting. The olive-colored Dr. 1 204/17 is another *Dreidecker* in the collection of the Technik Museum Speyer. *Fokker Team Schorndorf*

262

The olive-colored Dr. 1 204/17 is another *Dreidecker* in the collection of the Technik Museum Speyer. It was built by Hermann Ring from Ron Sands's plans, which were designed for the average homebuilder to be able to build a Fokker *Dreidecker* using limited space. Achim Engels visited Hermann and is seen inspecting Ring's triplane being built in his garage. He completed the airplane in 1992, and it is currently on display next to Engels's triplane. *Public domain*

The Military Aviation Museum

This museum has a flying collection that is also housed indoors as museum displays during nonflying weather. Museums such as Owls Head, Fantasy of Flight, and others also do this, which is an excellent year-round aspect of their collections. In addition to the all-red Richthofen paint scheme, this museum also has one in a refreshingly different scheme; that of Jasta 27's Rudolf Klimke's Dr. 1 577/17 (*opposite*). Klimke ended the war with seventeen victories. *Public domain*

CHAPTER 7
Flying Replica/Reproduction Fokker Dr. 1s

There are a few aerodromes in the United States and abroad where one can see a flying Dr. 1, although these aircraft are replicas or reproductions, and only a handful have the original power plant—a 110 hp rotary engine. These are demanding aircraft to fly, just as they were back in 1917, so all conditions must be right before they can rise skyward. These aircraft do not like excessive wind due to their high aspect, draggy airframe, and slow speed, so don't be too disappointed if you don't get to see one fly due to sudden changes in weather.

The Old Rhinebeck Aerodrome in New York, Golden Age Air Museum in Pennsylvania, Virginia Aviation Museum in Virginia Beach, and Owls Head Transportation Museum in Maine are four places in the eastern US where one can see replica or reproduction triplanes.

Moreover, there are many smaller flying clubs that have kit-built Dr. 1s that are also fun to watch. Out west, Planes of Fame Museum in Chino, California, has a flying Dr. 1. In Europe, if you are lucky enough to live in Sweden, you might catch a glimpse of Mikael Carlson's excellent Dr. 1 flying above the colorful terrain of this region. Mikael built and flies his Dr. 1 and D.VII, which are exact in every detail. Mikael attends many premier flying shows across Europe.

If you find yourself in New Zealand, the Omaka Aviation Heritage Center hosts many flying events. Most replicas differ from the originals in some fashion—usually the engine—since rotaries are sometimes difficult to obtain and maintain (finding spare parts poses a big problem). On the other hand, modern replicas benefit from modern covering materials, instrumentation, brakes, and, in some cases, steerable tail skids. However, nods to the present are a matter of personal taste and discretion among Dr. 1 builders, owners, and pilots.

Golden Age Air Museum
Bethel, Pennsylvania

The Golden Age Air Museum was established in 1997, and its mission is to entertain visitors and educate them about the early days of aviation through its special events and daily operations. The museum offers the chance to explore the past, come and learn how the early aviators flew and what they flew, and learn the lost art of early aircraft construction. Museum displays include full-size operational aircraft and automobiles, as well as displays of artifacts from aviation's golden age. Craftsmen are continually working on restoring new additions for the collection; this work is done in view of the visitors. Talk with the restoration volunteers and learn techniques and practices of early aircraft builders. *From the GAAM website*

The beautiful Dr. 1 built by Paul Daugherty at the Golden Age Air Museum in Bethel, Pennsylvania, is pictured here "in the bones" against the Pennsylvania countryside. Paul mentioned that his inspiration stemmed from seeing Cole Palen flying his triplane at the Old Rhinebeck Aerodrome as a youth. Paul used plans from Redfern and Ron Sands and sought input from Gary Sewall, Frank Murrin, and Achim Engels regarding the design and construction of his *Dreidecker*. He noted that the design and exact placement of the undercarriage had been a big problem with many replicas—citing that Dr. 1's ground-handling characteristics have received a bad rap due to problems with the landing-gear design of some of the available plans. Paul spent twenty months building his Dr. 1 and ten years thinking about how to operate the 80 hp Le Rhône rotary engine he had obtained for the project. *Golden Age Air Museum*

Paul's completed Dr. 1 painted in Lothar von Richthofen's colors. Lothar used the yellow coloring on his Dr. 1 as a reminder of his old regiment, Dragoner-Regiment von Bredlow No. 4. Manfred, Lothar's famous brother, described Lothar's tactics as being "impetuous, of rushing into combat without thinking." That being said, the *Rittmeister*'s ambitious younger brother racked up twenty-four victories in just over six weeks at Jasta 11. Paul Daugherty noted that first he painted his triplane in the standard-issue streaked olive camouflage scheme, then overpainting the yellow—just as Lothar would have done at the front. *Photo courtesy of GAAM; alt photo courtesy of Stephen Chapis*

Two breathtaking aerial shots of Paul Dougherty flying his replica of Lothar von Richthofen's *Dreidecker*. The rural Pennsylvania landscape stretches out below and beyond the colorful *Dreidecker* in the late-day sunlight. The brightly colored triplanes of JG 1 gave rise to the term "Flying Circus," such was the dazzling array of colors used by this group. Paul commented that the roll rate is not overly fast but is responsive, and that it requires a fair amount of forward stick to keep the plane level. It turns on a dime, and Paul tried the famous "skidding turn" as documented by Voss and others; Paul said, "OK—check, I've done that, but the plane shakes something fierce, so won't do that again!" The gyroscopic effect of the 80 hp Le Rhône was not that noticeable, Paul noted; of course, the original was 110 hp, and as such it would have been more so. Paul said that the elevator was most effective, and even though it has a tiny rudder, it is still very effective, and the ailerons were light and responsive. Diving the *Dreidecker* was surprising in that it was faster than expected. Like Carlson, Paul noted that the Dr. 1 is flown by pure feel. The best indicator if the engine is getting enough castor oil? Make sure the left lower wing is always coated with the stuff! *Photos courtesy of Stephen Chapis*

A close-up of the spinning Le Rhône 80 hp engine fitted to Paul's Dr. 1. The gyroscopic effect of this spinning engine gave both the Dr. 1 and the Sopwith Camel a pronounced hard turn to the right. Turning both planes to the left took more time. Many *Dreideckers* flying today do not have rotary engines, but for those that do, their pilots claim it isn't really a Dr. 1 unless it has one! *Photo courtesy of Stephen Chapis*

Old Rhinebeck Aerodrome
Red Hook, New York

Cole Palen founded the Old Rhinebeck Aerodrome in 1958, with a handful of airplanes and a dream. He built it into a world-renowned destination as America's first flying museum of antique aircraft. The Rhinebeck Aerodrome Museum was established in 1993 to continue Cole's legacy. Their mission is preserving, restoring, and flying the aircraft of the pioneers, World War I, and the golden age of aviation. Over sixty vintage aircraft, many antique automobiles and motorcycles, and related memorabilia are located in a classic small-town airport setting. The static display museum is open from May through October, and two different airshows are flown each Saturday and Sunday from mid-June through mid-October. ORA consists of a volunteer board of trustees, professional staff, and many volunteers, who do everything from restorations to mowing the runway. *From the ORA website*

An early black-and-white photo of Cole Palen's first Dr. 1 (that he built) "in the bones," ca. 1967. Note the face on the cowling, taking its inspiration from Werner Voss, who painted his cowling this way to remind him of the Japanese kites of his youth that were painted in a similar fashion. Cole Palen was the founder of and driving force for the Old Rhinebeck Aerodrome in Rhinebeck, New York.

FOKKER DR-1
TRIPLANE
MFG ANTHONY FOKKER. 1917
SPEED: 115 MPH
CLIMB: 1300 ft./min.
CEILING: 20,000 ft.
RANGE: 2.5 hrs.

HIGH MANEUVERABILITY &
RATE OF CLIMB. A FAVORITE
OF von RICHTHOFEN AND
OTHER GERMAN ACES.
THERE WERE 320 DR-1's
BUILT. HOWEVER, NO
ORIGINALS EXIST TODAY.

A familiar sight for those who visit ORA for its fabulous summer airshows: their current Dr. 1, which is painted in a hybridization of influences; some Richthofen—the all-red paint scheme; some Voss—the face on the cowling; the "heart in the cloud" is taken from Leutnant Willi Rosenstein of Jasta 40; the pig's hindquarters, depicted on the left side of the fuselage, are representative of the markings from Unteroffizier Karl Rau's triplane, also from Jasta 40. Finally, the black and white stripes on the horizontal tail surfaces and subwing are typical of aircraft flown in Jasta 6. It too has a nonrotary engine, for safety reasons and for ease of handling.

ORA's Dr. 1 airborne! The fine pilots of the Aerodrome really put the Fokker through her paces, by executing low-level passes, stall turns, and other mild aerobatics—everyone who visits leaves with a sense of awe and wonder at these magnificent machines and the artistry of the pilots of the Aerodrome. If you've never been, make it a point to visit ORA—you'll find yourself returning year after year.

A close-up of ORA's Dr. 1 making its way over the Duchess County countryside. The Aerodrome is located just a few miles from the Taconic Parkway, near Red Hook—a stone's throw from New York City and I-90.

Owls Head Transportation Museum
Owls Head, Maine

Founded in 1974, the Owls Head Transportation Museum is an operating, nonprofit museum with a strong focus on educational initiatives. Located on the Maine coast near the Knox County Regional Airport, the museum is a place where machines of a bygone era are celebrated through conservation, preservation, and demonstration. Unlike many transportation museums, the Owls Head Transportation Museum operates their collection of aircraft, ground vehicles, and engines at a number of special events conducted throughout the year. Care and maintenance of these historic vehicles requires the attention of a large volunteer workforce that, under the supervision of a professional staff, ensures that the collection is in operating condition. While the museum is open all year, the summer event season offers an unparalleled opportunity to see the collection in action during scheduled airshows and ground vehicle demonstrations. *Taken from the OHTM website*

OHTM's Dr. 1 replica in the bones—note that the top and bottom wings are mostly complete, since the rib webs have been secured and braced with fabric tape. The middle wing is still in progress, as evidenced by the lack of taping and a few ribs that appear unaligned. It was built by Ken Cianchette and donated to OHTM.

OHTM's Dr. 1 was finished in Manfred von Richthofen's all-red livery. Richthofen started painting his earlier triplanes only partly red; by the spring of 1918, he painted his Dr. 1 completely red in preparation for Operation Michael—the offensive upon which Germany pinned all its hopes of turning the tide of the war in its favor. Also pictured is a close-up of the engine in the reproduction— it is not a rotary, which makes for a more stable aircraft since it does not have the extreme gyroscopic effects of the original Oberursel II rotary engine.

Owl's Heads Dr. 1 just after breaking ground—note the slight up elevator and right rudder input. The Dr. 1 was extremely short coupled in all dimensions, making it very sensitive in the air and requiring concentration on takeoffs and landings.

OHTM's triplane on a flyover bathed in late-afternoon sunshine. Here the all-red paint scheme is very apparent; typically the undersides of the wings and fuselage were painted a sky blue.

Mikael Carlson's fabulous Dr. 1 "in the bones" in front his workshop and airfield in Sweden. Mikael had this to say about building and flying his Dr. 1: "I have the feeling that I have come as close to the original as possible, and it feels right for the machine to fly in a fantastic way. The first thing to learn is how to handle the engine as it is very powerful in relation to the weight of the plane." *Daniel Karlsson*

Carlson's Dr. 1 403/17 finished in the colors of Jasta 6's Johann Janzen. It is a beautiful specimen. Mikael commented that "The plane flies very well but must be flown all the time; you can never release the controls and there is no stability in any control axis. During takeoff roll, be careful to keep the course, and it is necessary to use deft rudder deflections and while climbing almost full right rudder." *Daniel Karlsson*

Carlson's Dr. 1 high over the Swedish landscape. "There are no flight instruments in the Dr. 1, only tachometer, compass, and fuel gauge, so it has to be flown with feeling all the time, and I tell you if there would have been an airspeed indicator, I would never look at it; the best instrument in a Dr. 1 is the feeling in your behind."
Daniel Karlsson

Banking steeply and at low level, Carlson prepares to land his *Dreidecker*. Regarding landing a Dr. 1, Mikael notes, "Finally, always land into the wind and always [make landings] three-point; ground roll on soft grass [is] about 70 meters." When asked why he builds and flies these wonderful aircraft, Mikael commented that "the reward is to recover lost knowledge and [to experience] the joy of being able to test it yourself and show it to people that otherwise only can see these planes in a museum, where they are dead and without soul. And also to bring color, sound, and smell to the old black-and-white photos you see of all these airplanes." Carlson noted that the passion he brings to flying and building his aircraft has taken him around the world three times—such is the interest in and appreciation for what he does.
Daniel Karlsson

Achim Engels is another impassioned perfectionist who has spent his life researching and building exacting replicas of Fokker aircraft. His organization, Fokker Team Schorndorf, is located in Schorndorf, Germany, and specializes in re-creating the aircraft of Anthony Fokker and his talented designers and engineers. Pictured here is the tube steel framework of Achim's beautiful Dr. 1, which is exact in every detail. It has the yellow rudder that would have been found on Lothar von Richthofen's *Dreidecker*. The sign hanging on the wall, "Halle 2," actually came from the remains of the old Fokker factory in Schwerin.

The austere yet beautiful cockpit of Achim's Dr. 1. Note the tachometer, compass, ammo magazine, and functional yet adjustable seat of the *Dreidecker*. Also note the stick and its interesting grip, which includes triggers for both machine guns and a throttle level on the left. The "blip switch" is the white button atop the stick—this allows the pilot to cut off the engine and control speed by means of engine pulses. The U-shaped forks are where the breeches of the twin machine guns are fitted. Note the antichafing tape that is wrapped around turnbuckles and framing to prevent the metal from abrading the fabric covering.

A close-up of the starboard side of the cockpit, showing the distressed metal turtle deck cowling, machine guns, and box spar and trailing edge of the middle wing. The crossed rigging that supports the cabane struts, combined with a similar bracing of the landing gear, is the extent of the rigging on a Dr. 1. This lack of flying wires, and the subsequent drag they produce, contributes to the surprising speed mentioned by Paul Daugherty of the *Dreidecker*.

Another view of the turtle deck neatly enclosing the middle wing of the Dr. 1. Also visible is the thin, plywood, "sawtooth" leading-edge sheeting that was a signature feature of Fokker aircraft. A signature feature of Achim Engels's aircraft is excellent craftsmanship and exacting attention to detail.

Chris Hill commented that "I was first drawn into this era when I read the Red Baron's autobiography at about ten years old while staying with my grandmother, a librarian, during the summer. By the time I finished the book, I was a Red Baron fan, and it stuck with me for the rest of my life." Chris says, "It stands out in my mind as a symbol of aerial prowess, wielded by masters of aerial combat and the World War I ace of aces himself, Manfred von Richthofen. For that reason, I sought a chance to fly this plane, the king of the dogfight."

Chris's Fokker Dr. 1, 239/17, was built in Connecticut by Jim Bruton. Chris was very pleased with Bruton's job on the plane and was "exceedingly grateful" that Jim sold it to him. Chris stated that "Jim successfully made his first flight in the Dr. 1 with 100 hours [of] total time and just three hours of tailwheel time, a feat I would say requires a lot of luck and a healthy dose of skill, as 239/17 has neither brakes nor a tailwheel, which is a foreign concept to anyone learning to fly today." Chris commented that "239/17 is a historical-fiction paint scheme. Jim Bruton combined elements of other historical Fokker Dr. 1 schemes to arrive at what is on the plane." Chris went on to say that "239/17 is in the serial number gap during the time when the Dr. 1 was grounded. There never was a real Fokker Dr. 1 with the serial 239/17. The serial holds significance for Jim due to his favorite World War I pilot being Werner Voss, whose last flight was September 23, 1917 (239/17). The cowling is painted in the colors of Jasta 2, the black and white stripes resemble that of Ernst Udet's Dr. 1, and the cross on the tail was also painted on several Dr. 1s."

On flying the Fokker triplane, Chris likes to say, "It is a pilot's airplane! When you fly it, you always have something to do. It requires both feet, both hands, and a little prayer. It lacks stability in all axes, where relinquishing the controls, for even a fraction of a second, results in instantaneous wild pitching and yawing that will put you on your back if left uncorrected. If you want a stable airplane that trims up and flies hands off, this one isn't even close. To some, that might sound like a lot of work to fly a plane around, and I would agree in large part. However, if you have an aviator's soul and the sky beckons you, this is the most exhilarating ride you can take aloft. It will test your mind, body, and spirit. The Fokker triplane loves to fly, though. It will pitch and roll and yaw at your slightest command. It stalls in a flat descent, akin to coming down in a parachute, and it loops so tight that I fear I may inadvertently chop off my own tail with the propeller."

Colorful triplanes gather at the Omaka Aviation Heritage center in New Zealand every year. This group of *Dreideckers* has chosen to paint their planes in the bright coloring of Richthofen's famous "Flying Circus." Classic Fighters Omaka air show is held over three days from Good Friday to Easter Sunday every alternate year, as a major fundraising event for the Omaka Aviation Heritage Centre. The main show days are Saturday and Sunday, with the program running from approximately 10:00 a.m. to 4:00 p.m.

Endnotes

Chapter 1

1. At least one triplane was tested with the 110 hp Le Rhône rotary engine, with negligible positive results.

2. J. M. Bruce, *The Sopwith Triplane* (London: Profile Publications, 1966), 4.

3. Ibid.

4. Clayton & Shuttleworth built six triplanes with twin guns, but the increase in weight and subsequent reduction in flight performance marginalized their efficacy.

Chapter 2

1. Tomasz J. Kowalski, *Pfalz—Fighter Aircraft: From Rheinland the Wine Country* (Lublin, Poland: Kagero, 2013), 13.

2. Ibid., 15.

3. Ibid.

Chapter 3

1. The drag of its three wings acted as a brake in a steep dive; biplanes would generate greater speeds, leading to wing shearing or disintegration.

2. Alex Imrie, *The Fokker Triplane* (London: Arms and Armour, 1992), 25.

3. Ibid., 27.

Chapter 5

1. He was joined at some point by a red-nosed Albatros; see Norman Franks and Greg VanWyngarden, *Fokker Dr 1 Aces of World War I* (Oxford: Osprey, 2001), 18.

2. James McCudden. *Five Years in the Royal Flying Corps* (London: Aeroplane and General Publishing, 1918), 176.

3. Franks and VanWyngarden, *Fokker Dr 1 Aces of World War I*, 69.

4. Jacobs once referred to this insignia as a "fire spitting witch"; see Franks and WynGarden, *Fokker Dr 1 Aces of World War I*, 72.

Bibliography

Bruce, J. M. *The Fokker Dr. 1*. London: Profile Publications, 1965.

Bruce, J. M. *The Sopwith Triplane*. London Profile Publications, 1966.

Franks, Norman, and Greg VanWyngarden. *Fokker Dr 1 Aces of World War I*. Oxford: Osprey, 2001.

Imrie, Alex. *The Fokker Triplane*. London: Arms and Armour, 1992.

Kowalski, Tomasz J. *Pfalz—Fighter Aircraft: From Rheinland the Wine Country*. Lublin, Poland: Kagero, 2013.

McCudden, James. *Five Years in the Royal Flying Corps*. London: Aeroplane and General Publishing, 1918.